No True Route

Tim Conroy

No True Route

Tim Conroy

No True Route.

Copyright 2023 by Tim Conroy. All Rights Reserved.

Printed in the United States of America. No parts of the book may be reproduced in any manner without written permission except in the case of brief quotations embodied in critical articles or reviews.

Library of Congress Control Number: 2023947136

ISBN: 978-1-942081-39-5

Cover photography by Kathleen Robbins.

Dedication

To my verdant dreamer and loyalist,
Terrye McKenzie Conroy

Being with you, and not being with you, is the only way I have to measure time.

Jorge Luis Borges

Contents

Foreword
No True Route

I.

The Great Ravine
Road Trip
Lousy
Crab Trap
Premeditation
Unstable Air
Backyard Church
Misdirection
Paws

II.

Blue Corvair
Dandelion
Fibs
Centering
Key
Promise Things
Home Fires
Movie Heroes
The Heart is an Eye
Soup with Nothing
Nothing Stays Swept
A Military Brat's Goodbyes

Ballade for the Remaining Years
Horseshoes

III.

Navigation
Last Call
Swallow the Why
What Blinded Eyes
CRT
Baby Blues
Circus
Untrained Mule
Panorama
Journeys

IV.

Her Birthday
Destination
My Dog at the Beach
Shells for a Jar
What's Kept Remembers You
Bend
UnShelled
Visitations

Epigraph

When all is said and done,
we're all just walking each other home.

Ram Dass

Foreword

Where have you been? How did you get here? Where are you going?

The title of Tim Conroy's second book, No True Route, asks us to think about journeys in both time and space. Throughout the book, poems take up themes of movement, direction, detour, destination. And they take up those inevitable moments we pause and look back, asking how we got here, surveying those landscapes of time and family in loss in which nothing is static or reliable, especially memory. What were the signposts? Where could this life have taken another direction? What then? Who would I have been? Who would he have been? Not this man, certainly. Another, perhaps harder, or lost, and not a writer. We all do this, sometimes, think about the choices we made or failed to make, the inheritances we rejected and those we kept, like a mother's jar of seashells on a bookshelf, a slight thing, a thing weighted with memory, with the inevitabilities of choices made.

I'm struck, though, reading this book again, by a theme of sustenance that threads the book—a mother packing her children's lunches, a joke between spouses about a soup of nothing, coastal meals of crab and shrimp, a bag of chips that rivets a dog's attention. Or dreams that will be eaten. Rainwater in chalices. Surely that is another way to think about our lives: the things and people that have sustained us, fed us, kept us going.

And surely that is another way to think about poetry like this. Something to chew on. Something that can keep us going. Words that sustain.

Ed Madden, August 2023

No True Route

Merge or stop,
left or right,
departure or arrival—

you need directions
from strangers
for inward destinations too.

I.

The Great Ravine

Would you have ever guessed
that you would make it to the other side
of the great ravine?
Why did you cross in high winds?
Why did you tiptoe to the middle
and dangle on one foot?
Why did you have to juggle those swords?
Aren't you suspicious of the knots?
How many others have you witnessed fall
inching along in perfect weather?
Fool heart, daredevil, spender of your one life,
what were you thinking, and why
have you started to cross back in the freezing rain?
Why do you laugh when I say it's not safe?
Are you singing?

Road Trip

On a dark road, sing loudly
and don't harmonize
with a chorus of shadows.

Don't circle back.
It's a roundabout anyway,
the universe travels fast.

Pile on more mileage
and drive your wreck.
It's a jalopy pilgrimage.

When your tire bursts,
love the strangers
that fix the flats.

Lousy

My Dad said lousy a lot
to describe his children
a lousy jump shot, a lousy right fielder,
a lousy bedmaker, a lousy dishwasher,
with a lousy attitude.

We had lousy eyes, freckles, and postures.

But he would never admit,
we were stationed in lousy towns.
We could have become lousy
because he fought in three lousy wars,
where he won a few lousy medals.

Every year, we left friends and moved
on lousy cross-country car trips.
He had a lousy temper and backhand.
His world turned lousier when our mom divorced him.
He was lousy in love with her.
He tasted lousy when schizophrenia
came for one of his sons.

Afterward, he was never a lousy grandfather
or a lousy money giver.
He remained lousy at saying sorry.

When he died, we never felt lousier
and knew a pilot's love didn't land empty,
his caps and his godawful shirts,
his lousy flaws, our hearts.

Crab Trap

My tidal river, the river inside,
brings me back to hold
the rope knotted to adolescence
not far from the sea pass.
What draws us to currents?

Underneath every coastal dock
is a boy stuck in a crab trap
with dreams that crawl and pinch,
and wait to be eaten.

Premeditation

On the drive to the Braves' game,
he bellowed; *There's a hammer under the seat
in case we need to brain someone.*

I towed him up ramps, hip worn
with his throttle hand across my shoulder.
He would kill for me and one more hot dog.

I felt his warrior's grip when I
lifted myself above—nothing like him.
He didn't give a crap about effort, just results.

He flew Corsairs in the Korean war
landed sinister wings on rolling seas
& taught me to keep box scores.

Unstable Air

Even with the unpredictable winds
the unstable air
springtime has never been more beautiful.
A young rat snake
slithers from the fig tree
at the fence line
disappears by the butterfly bush.

Heat has not yet flickered
its thick wet tongue.
All the sounds of spring
have the aroma of the jasmine
clambering over the fence.

The cheers, stolen verses, sweet tea songs
of towhee, sparrow, wren, thrasher
in an orchestra more aligned
than heart, body, lung.
There is hope in our diminishment.

Has it ever been more clear
we must cease
what we are doing?
And we must try to do
the thing as natural
as resting wings to heal
a broken bone, pandemic, torn spirit.

Backyard Church

When you worship
weeds you can't name
with pews full of bees

When you worship
the procession of zebras to the jasmine

When you worship
squirrels chattering morning gospels
and turtles praying in garden temples

When you worship
spiders that hang white robes
on stained-glass branches
and the skink that rose from the dead

There's the new congregation of red shoulder bugs

There's rainwater in green chalices

Do you recall the moment you first belonged?

Misdirection
after Ralph Albert Blakelock's *Moonlight*

1
There is a moment of disbelief
in every disappearing act — a stunned silence
as you rub your eyes.

2
The trees lean for a look,
did the little girl fall
behind the curtain?

3
Who among us isn't mesmerized
by grief's dark waters,
silvering the sky at moonlight?

4
We gasp at what's revealed.
A floating pail, a plastic shovel.
Nothing else.

Paws

thirst hangs from his tongue
ears twitch at the ripped bag of chips
the dark mirth of eyes
ready to pounce the distance
nudge you to explore instincts
where there are no saviors, lords, masters
only breeds that pant for the torn

II.

Blue Corvair

My fighter pilot Pop
flew a blue Corvair
raced his ragtop hot—

never air-cooled.
His temper, God's speed
inside a phantom heart.

It takes guts
to comprehend a mother
isn't built to rescue anyone.

Dandelion

Not when your father threatened stitches
not when the silent movers unloaded
not when boxes were unpacked
not when you dribbled off squared away
from elephants, floor-to-ceiling lamps,
brass tables, trinkets, and tapestries.
It's when the first kid from town
throws a death kiss to a dandelion
did the military brat move in.

Fibs

When my mother died,
what became of her fantasies?
She struggled through
roaring jets and landing strips,
dismal apartments,
her hysterectomy one Nebraskan winter.

Snowjobs piled high
slant—purity. She told
whoppers to the other wives
a degree from Agnes Scott,
the Pope's blessing in Italy,
my favorite as she melted,
he was a loving man.

It never crossed our minds
she would die before Dad.
It's not too late to create
little fibs to fool ourselves
when she lied, I loved
her truthful eyes.

Centering

We focus on their shoulders, their labored breath, their puffed
face in a centering of support.

We adjust and center them in bed and center the room
with blessings.

We administer morphine to center their pain.

We sponge them with warm water for fresh centerings.

We focus on the kitchen's centering smells
of rotisserie chicken and casseroles.

We collapse into desperate centers as dogs and children
howl for us to gather our resolve.

When they slip into the mysterious center, we keep
their unmated sock in the center of our drawer.

Key

No one predicts the instant you forget
or how a body holds a soul's regret.
We rise, we weep, and lose the key
to unlock this grief-filled room.

Promise Things

after Otto Neuman's *Head and Shoulders of a Woman*

Who are we to judge? Men
and women promise things
never fully knowing
what they mean.

He left her after forty years,
said the blame was hers,
she'd derailed his dreams
another would redeem.

Whether it was sadness or uncertainty,
she transformed—,
abstracted from her former self,
chiseled smooth.

Home Fires

Fresh cut, as kids
we were thrown
into the pits
of our home fires.

Under a blanket in the back seat of a
'57 Chevy, she hid as her father
pressed a snub-nose
against her mother's temple,
while my dear-ole'-dad
smashed my buzz-cut against the walls
of military housing.

Years later, therapeutically tipsy,
we met. Deprived of oxygen
until she answered, I asked her out.
First date—we sat cross-legged
in a ballroom, serenaded
by the Swimming Pool Qs,
our eyes babbled.

In the wee hours, we sat
in a train station diner eating pancakes,
swapping passages from a short stack
of syrupy Westerns left on the ledge along our booth.

Bad guys all vanquished—

we flew open the doors of her Corolla—our Conestoga.
Each stuck out a leg
to ease it in reverse.
A team, plodding backward
out of blind canyons
to face a rocky trail.

When we finally kissed,
We swore to hell as lovers
not to bank fire.
And prayed
that a blazing hearth
would take us both to ash.

Movie Heroes
after Steven Naifeh's *Saida X: Chrome*

Dad came back tanked.
Mom voiced displeasure.
When he backhanded her,
he sputtered on the deck.

I watched my movie heroes,
Butch and Sundance jump.

Raindrops fell on my head.
I lost my laughter.
Maybe all boys do.

We ran and locked the car
thinking we were safe.
Rattling—Jingling—
he had an extra set of keys.
We gave up.

The Heart is an Eye

Sometimes the heart is an eye
that sees the trouble coming.
Sometimes it's a lump of flesh
pumping sand through the hours—
numb as any empty liquor bottle

tossed away. Other times it's a star
that everything revolves around
brighter than a supermoon over water.
It grabs the mic and sings.

When I think I understand it, I don't.

And I can't explain
the inexplicable pluck of its center.
It throws itself into trouble headfirst,
even when it flutters in fear.

It breaks over the littlest things,
a sad flower stuck in a crack,
a dog's warm lick.
When shunned, it hides for years.

But when it falls in love, it unbodies. Floats.

Soup with Nothing
after Raphael Soyer's *Entering the Studio*

She asks if I would like
soup mit nisht—
a jest between us.
Moments, non-spectacular,
leave us speechless.

The harmonious colors
of her blouse
in front of austere walls
bring me to her hands.
Hands that hold.

It's the flavoring—
the softness around her eyes,
the light on a grandmother
overlooking children
playing on the sidewalk.

These images are as authentic
as the distances we cross
when we sip soup together.
Nothing warmer.
Nothing as nourishing.

Nothing Stays Swept

Each year, we peel fresh
on barrier islands
with polka-dotted cheer
in the undertow of letdowns.

We drain coffee,
eat buffet style, then pee
and pee until nothing's left.
Nothing stays swept.

We slather and wear sunhats
march in pecking order
veer in unison
to marvel at comebacks.

We flip-flop narratives
devein each other
sauté another year
in the blend of reunion.

A Military Brat's Goodbyes

I dared not belly ache to annual moving vans,
to smells of freshly made cardboard boxes,
to miles of bubble wrap and rolls of packing tape,
to crewcuts on bicycles circling the block,
to roars of stop yacking, bedtime, and predawn reveille,
to last rites for the sacrament of urination,
to belted renditions of *She'll be coming around the mountain*,
to Stuckeys and rest stops passed by, to deadly car farts
and wicked elbows, to entryways of dandelions,
unconquerable fast-food signs, surrendered strip malls
and bombed-out motels,
the blue milieu of military towns.

Years later my emotions dug trenches
at plastic smiles, salutes, slow waves of wrists—
the pretense of departures. I panicked each mile closer
to holiday gatherings and family beach trips.
I blamed my wife for potholes and blind spots
till she confronted me with plainspoken medicine—
snap out of it, idiot.
Meanwhile the boy inside me was marching away,
under house arrest or confounded by invention.
The lie of a comprehensible family, of a mythical father,
of a believable mother, of good-natured ease
and accountings.

It was Mike and Kathy who posited the Family Bell Curve:
sane simpletons, average dumb fucks, batshit crazies.
If I drank enough, the curve would choose
and if I lied enough, it became a game.
I tried to transform into an artful listener
to reject the altar of make-believe.

I toasted Sunbeam bread,
uttered non-committal, waited, nodded,
and questioned to fool my mouth from revealing
wounds below hand-me-down unraveling sweaters.
I hid my bedwetter's journal with its rage of freckles and
hazel eyes, its record of wounded moments
in kitchens where we became complicit.

Worse, we acted normal to ruin ourselves.
His yearly orders were my chance to find the lost boy,
child, pre-teen, adolescent, and almost clear-eyed man
and for a while it would work until a Father
slapped a Mother across rooms and we stood paralyzed
in a military family's good posture.
A family photo so posed it scorched tongues into silence.
Memories flicker with dark flames,
and some basements have cold furnaces.
Truth's more potent than love; it never hides.
Unpack, tell—say goodbyes.

Ballade for the Remaining Years

"Call hospice in," says Dr. Biggs,
  Nurses shrug from what they know.
You fortify with burning swigs,
  Lose your mind and act composed.
When death is sudden and unposed,
  It's agony and bitter strife,
But don't toss out their comfy clothes.
  Invoke the dead into your life.

Wind chimes and the whirligigs,
  Finches singing by the rose,
Reminders by the herbal sprigs
  The silences of where God goes.
Ashes that the families throw,
  Stab like granulated knives.
How do you let grief transpose?
  Invoke the dead into your life.

Mom's apron by the jar of figs
  Some stains are lovely, you suppose
Forget the chemo and the wig.
  The descant notes of organ blows
Preacher's gaffes and blurry rows
  The memories that wreck a wife,
Don't hide the photo on the shelf.
  Invoke the dead into your life.

Loneliness parades their shadows,
With tearful fits and wailing fife.
Chitchat to them when feeling low,
Invoke the dead into your life.

Horseshoes

One month ago
an oak limb fell
yet not until this moment
did you pick it up.

It fits perfectly
to strong-knee a wardrobe
from tipping in your truck.

Circles of circles
circling
chance encounters.

Everyone comes back
to clang
horseshoes together.

Every face a dead ringer—
friend, sibling, father, or mother.

III.

Navigation

Before sailing offshore
examine murky water struck out of blue
study the flight of skimmers and hourglass sandbars
watch porpoises herding mullet to mudflat demise
drink starlit motion kissed by lipless water
mourn whey-faced trees swallowed by tides
mark the set and drift of your resolve

Last Call

Twenty years ago
I rang the bell, yelled last call,
saw familiar faces fall.
Another trip
on a concrete floor
to mix up more
to say goodnight
to thank them all for coming.
Food and beverage folk
winding down from a frantic shift
tipping more
than they could afford.

I met friends
at the bar.
One soul
bought the bar a shot to toast
a friend who passed
the week before.
There are moments
when it burns you more.

I wiped the sticky bar
with soda water
and poured more.
As the last group left,
I counted tips and surveyed
the spillage of a single day.

I met friends
more than halfway down the bar.
One soul
bought the bar a shot to toast
a friend who passed
the week before.

There are moments
when it burns you more.

Swallow the Why

I fly into a crowded bar,
a half-full street, a labyrinth
make such inglorious choices
and wonder why I landed there.

Mostly, I swallow the why
buzz to whoever will listen.
The clerk of lost screws at Ace Hardware,
the membership checker at Costco,
and the ex-con at Stan's carwash
make me believe I am part
of how we are connected.

But after a few hasty turns,
I'm stuck behind the blinds again.

What Blinded Eyes

When Sgt. Isaac Woodard was discharged in 1946
and road a bus home to South Carolina,
I was not born and had no eyes for him.

When Sgt. Woodard still in uniform
asked the driver to use the washroom,
and reasoned "I am a man just like you,"
I was not born and had no eyes for him.

When the police chief of Batesburg
blackjacked Sgt. Woodard's eyes to craters,
I was not born and had no eyes for him.

And when Jim Crow America saw
African American World War II veterans
pin their medals to ragdoll jobs,
I was not born and had no eyes for them.

But what of my sight now?

I never viewed myself as the white
bus driver angered at how Sgt. Woodard
held his gaze and liberated himself.

I never viewed myself as the white
soldier who did nothing
when Sgt. Woodard was ordered off the bus.
And I never viewed myself as the white

police chief who gouged Sgt. Woodard's eyes
and bloodied him.

Though I must see I am them—
privileged, obedient, blind
turning off the latest lynching on TV
never doing enough— not then, not now.

CRT

all the sea—a drowned history book

enslaved people revolted on ships
pages bound, ripped

later pinned with monstrous wings
scared poor whites to death

stole black lives back by lynching them
burned black towns to black smoke
paved over black graveyards

cut string for the rest
to measure feet for shoes
since they could not enter stores

scattered across the seafloor, bookmarks

Baby Blues
Elegy for my brother Tom

His baby blues are floating fish
The college freshman ruptures time
In search of his autonomy
Psychotic breaks are hard to fix

The college freshman ruptures time
Psychotic breaks are hard to fix
His friends are doubles after him
Avoids his siblings to hold firm

Psychotic breaks are hard to fix
Avoids his siblings to hold firm
Deceitful shadows roam about
Their clannish faces menace him

Avoids his siblings to hold firm
Their clannish faces menace him
They fret about new episodes
He's taken in through trickery

Their clannish faces menace him
He's taken in through trickery
To meet the chief psychiatrist
In thirty days released with pills

He's taken in through trickery
In thirty days released with pills

At night in parks, he sulks alone
His inklings are afraid of him

In thirty days released with pills
His inklings are afraid of him
To silence thoughts, it's Jameson
He hides the pills to find himself

His inklings are afraid of him
He hides the pills to find himself
The rooftop demons amplify
In search of his autonomy

He hides the pills to find himself
In search of his autonomy
A schizophrenic takes a dive
His baby blues are floating fish

Circus
after Walt Kuhn's *Outdoor Circus*

I clasp the hands of Phillipe
leap, and he lifts me
above his head in one motion.

With my feet together,
I mimic the angle of arches
until a town surrounds my spine.

I concentrate on the couple
with the small child
or the old man's beret.

From this held view
with quivering arms
in the clarity of compression,
I feel the crowd twinge.

I bend more
until I'm close to you
until we're all acrobats
held up by someone—

the extraordinary feat of how
not to be a body
suspended alone.

Untrained Mule

The untrained mule knocks you down
on your homestead island.
It's not ingenuity that saves you,
but the sea oats change direction.
The universe suddenly dizzy
with swirling bioluminescence
hermit crabs, ospreys, or burrowing owls
distract the hooves from crashing down
on this fragile life.

Panorama

I can't help but notice
pandemonium follows pandemic
in the Oxford Reference Dictionary.

And who's to blame
when *panic* finishes the column?
Don't linger over infectious fright.

I slide two fingers up to pancake,
stick to how Mimi sizzled
dollar-sized ones and drenched
me in buttery hope and syrup.

I bring my elbow down on pang
for elderly neighbors,
sudden sharp uncertainty
considers Pandora's box.

I look up and root for panda,
tumbling ageless wonder.
The one we love, China loaned to us.

Journeys

And I have sought a mountainous view
 until the altitude confused me.
And I've wandered off the path
 and was trapped in a storm
 without a map or provisions.
I should never have set out alone
—cold the stone of self-recrimination
 but inexplicably, hope appears
 in the trickle, then the river.
Unsure I stagger onward
 through the fog
 until the astonishment of falls
 the roar of brokenness and strength
 how a journey ends.

IV.

Her Birthday

Mom's birthday comes
in early January, and I shiver
surprised by how much I think of her
since most of her life
I didn't think of her enough.
I never understood her mystery
inside my school lunch
in a brown paper bag
that I carried and still carry
when I gather with my siblings
to laugh around the table.
Baloney and Sunbeam bread,
Duke's and a dab of yellow mustard,
iceberg lettuce and, if lucky,
a piece of sharp cheddar
cut in half and wrapped
with hands that took the time to seal
the way a mother nourishes.
When January lays me bare,
I remember she fed me royal caviar.

Destination

There's time to reach your destination
even if you take a moment to examine
what the buzzards are unraveling—
their slow flap of air.

When you pass a ramshackle cabin
with rockers on the porch
and a rusted pickup in the field,
stop, get out, and amble

down the path to the creek,
spot the kingsnake.
Lounge shoeless on the flat rock,
and wiggle your toes.

My Dog at the Beach

I spot my dog chasing terns.
It chews a corner off the horizon.
I call to those that are lost.
How this dog has taken my grief
like a shell in its mouth. My plea,
a sharp note on the wind.
More than any person deserves,
it brings me a dead fish.

Shells for a Jar

Her blue eyes seek
shells for a keepsake jar
in the unbound sand
the oceans of torment
no longer churning
from a stormy marriage.
Her horizon bright
with a new husband
on their dream beach.
Now her shells on my shelf
conjure the collection
of wives who have found
ones full of imperfections
until finally, the worthy keeper.
She died at 59—waves crashing.

What's Kept Remembers You

We bought the desk at the store near the beach
and no matter where we live, I hear the waves.
The stapler I stole walks me into my favorite teacher.
An apron I hang on the closet door
takes me to the restaurant where I bartended.
The list includes an old bedside lamp,
and when I turn it on, I hear my Dad
yell at me to turn it off.
The books on the shelf are chapters of my life.
I don't have room for all the memories.
Things have gone quiet except for an old postcard
from a friend who died.

Bend
For B.M, A.M., and K.R.

In mourning's filtered light,
follow a marked path home

on freshly fallen petals
to report the tragic news

that we must be kind
and watchful as we pass.

There's time
to cut the neighbor's grass.

Everything he knew of love,
he left for us,

we need only bend
to pick it up.

Unshelled

I have come back to a place
where the blue heron calls
on a bluff over a tidal river
surrounded by towering oaks
along twisted squirrel roads
through hanging grey tunnels
what my years have wrought
unshelled in the pluff
with the spartina quivering
to invisible hands
cupped ripples of sunlight
sway with the river
the sunset's colors
wash me where water passes
to the stunned stillness of next tides
and oyster cuts of memories
mix with salt water
for a kind of resurrection
around the next bend
knowing home is the place
emerging from this river

Visitations

After the sheriff tracked you down in the cabin in the Great Smokies and said your father was gone, you took the winding drive to be alone and saw him waiting in the bend, surprised he would appear so soon. The old buck nodded to tell you what he could never say aloud. You never felt more like a part of him. And when your mother died surrounded by outstretched hands, you spied the black snake a week later disappearing into the mimosa, and you didn't have to see where it went; it was enough that it moved silently to do things that a mother must do. And when your younger brother chose death, and your older brother died of living too hard, they appeared together above Damascus as you hiked in the snow and spotted two ponies running like brothers, the younger pretending to be slower but chasing the other. Each threw kindred eyes at you until they disappeared over the hill, leaving tracks to follow, knowing one day, you will appear across a field and stare at someone who will rejoice at the heart of a wild creature.

Acknowledgments

To Phillip, the best father; Lindsay, the best mother; and Jackson, the best son I know.

To my siblings and their spouses and their love and laughter through our circle of time: Carol, Mike and Jean, Kathy and Bobby, and Jim and Janice.

To Cassandra King Conroy, who shows us how Great Love persists.

To the family spread across the map: Jessica, Bill, Elise, Lonny, Aurora Skye, Stella, Melissa, Jay, Lila, Joseph, Megan, Molly, Jack, Katie, Susannah, Rachel, Andy, Henry, Audrey, Michael, Willie, Laura, Coda, and Jasper. To Barbara Conroy, who I can never thank enough. Without them, there are no welcome stations, signposts, or mileage markers.

To my cathedral of friends, roadside saviors, bartenders, random saints, revolutionaries, listeners, poetry lovers, teachers, seekers, and doubters who have helped me on my pilgrimage.

To the writers, artists, and poets who continue to fuel me, especially Al Black, Clifford Brooks, Stephen Chesley, Anne Creed, Carla Damron, Curtis Derrick, Jonathan Hannah, Miho Kinnas, J. Drew Lanham, Ed Madden, Michael Miller, Phillip Mullen, Joe Palmer, Kathleen Robbins, Maggie Schein, and Marjory Wentworth.

To the mentors like Jonathan Haupt who take the time to encourage others to find their words.

To independent bookstores and libraries that save us one book at a time.

To Cindi Boiter and Bob Jolley and their advocacy for the literary arts. To Ed Madden, gifted editor and remarkable poet. I can never praise them enough.

To Dr. William Dufford for his guidance, friendship, and untiring support of social and environmental justice.

To the affirming and inclusive humans doing the work of love at Faith UCC in Dunedin, Florida.

To the Pat Conroy Literary Center in Beaufort, S.C., and its effort to connect writers and poets with communities of readers.

To Kathleen Robbins, Asher Madden, and the memory of Ben Madden.

To my dearly departed family: Peggy, Don, Pat, and Tom.

To the memory of Deborah and Jerrye.

And always to Terrye, who finds me when I'm lost.

Notes

"Dandelion" was written for my lifelong friends Scott, Alan, and Amy Basnett.

A version of "Key" was presented at Stormwater studio in response to K. Wayne Thornley's *Things She Carried*, a mixed media assemblage.

"Untrained Mule" was written in response to *Yesteryear I Lived in Paradise: The Story of Caladesi* by Myrtle Scharrer Betz.

Versions of "Circus," "Misdirection," "Promise Things," "Movie Heroes," and "Soup with Nothing" were presented and recorded for the Columbia Museum of Art's *Write Around Series* in November (2018) as part of a project spearheaded by award winning poet Ray McManus.

"What Kept Remembers You" is dedicated to Anita Gotwals and Geoffrey Graves.

"Visitations" was inspired by conversations around the dinner table with Chuck, Pam, Carrie, and Bonifacio.

Editor Acknowledgments

I am grateful to the editors of the following publications where these poems first appeared.

"No True Route" was first included in a poetry project led by Ed Madden, the former poet laureate of Columbia, South Carolina, and supported by One Columbia for the Arts. "No True Route" was published in my collection, *Theologies of Terrain*, 2017.

A version of "Home Fires" appeared in *Fall Lines: a literary convergence* Volume V. (2018).

A version of "Last Call" appeared in *Blue Mountain Review*, Issue 11 (2018).

A version of "Horseshoes" appeared in *Poetry on the Comet*, selected by Ed Madden, former Poet Laureate for Columbia, South Carolina (2020).

"Panorama" appeared in the *Charleston Post and Courier,* a project spearheaded by Adam Parker and Marjory Wentworth in April (2020).

A version of "Unstable Air" appeared in *Sheltered*, a journal published by the Jasper Project featuring South Carolina artists responding to the pandemic.

A version of "Military Brat's Goodbyes" appeared in *Twelve Mile Review* Spring/Summer (2021).

A version of "What Blinded Eyes" appeared in *Ukweli: Searching for Healing Truth*, a book of essays and poems edited by Horace Mungin and Herb Frazier (2022). Details of Sgt. Isaac Woodard's blinding originated from the true account, *Unexampled Courage, The Blinding of Sgt. Isaac Woodard and the Awakening of President Harry S. Truman and Judge J. Waties Waring* by Judge Richard Gergel. "What blinded eyes…" is after a line found in "Staggerlee Wonders" by James Baldwin.

A version of "Backyard Church" appeared in *Fall Lines: a literary convergence* Volume IX (2022).

Drafts of "Her Birthday," "My Dog at the Beach," and "Unshelled" first appeared in Al Black's *Mind Gravy's Facebook Group*, created for poets to share works in progress. (2023).

About the Cover Artist

Kathleen Robbins was born in Washington, D.C. and raised in the Mississippi Delta. As a photographer, she examines the intersection of memory, grief, and our physical relationship to the natural world. Her photographs have been widely published and exhibited in solo and group exhibitions in galleries and museums, including The Halsey Institute of Contemporary Art and the Ogden Museum of Southern Art. She was the recipient of the 2011 PhotoNOLA Review Prize for her project *Into the Flatland*, which was published as a monograph in 2015. Robbins resides in Columbia, SC, where she is a professor of art, coordinator of the photography program and affiliate faculty of southern studies at the University of South Carolina. You can view more of her work at kathleenrobbins.studio.

About the Author

Tim Conroy is a poet and former educator. His work has appeared in *Fall Lines, Blue Mountain Review, Jasper Magazine, Marked by the Water, Sheltered, The Pulpwood Queens Celebrate 20 Years, Twelve Mile Review, Limelight, Poetry on the Comet, The Post and Courier, Ukweli: Searching for Healing Truth*, and *Our Prince of Scribes: Writers Remember Pat Conroy*. In 2017, Muddy Ford Press published Tim's first book of poetry, *Theologies of Terrain*, edited by Ed Madden. In 2022, he received the Broad River Prize for prose from *Fall Lines: a literary convergence* Volume IX. A founding board member of the Pat Conroy Literary Center established in his brother's honor, Tim and his wife Terrye live in Dunedin, Florida.

www.ingramcontent.com/pod-product-compliance
Lightning Source LLC
Chambersburg PA
CBHW041131110526
44592CB00020B/2769